© 2006 Assouline Publishing
601 West 26th Street, 18th floor
New York, NY 10001, USA
Tel.: 212 989-6810   Fax: 212 647-0005
www.assouline.com

Translation from the Spanish by Lambe y Nieto.

Photoengraving by Gravor (Suisse)
Printed by Grafiche Milani (Italy)

ISBN: 2 84323 868 4

LLADRÓ®

MERCEDES MARTÍNEZ MORENO

ASSOULINE

t he law of fate that embraces all other laws, and that is as inaccessible as the very source from which life emanates, is the patina glossing the history of the brothers Juan, José, and Vicente Lladró, the heroes of a singular adventure that has made their surname synonymous with virtuosity. Their brand has reached world leadership in the field of decorative porcelain sculpture in less than fifty years—an unprecedented feat and an extraordinary history.

Lladró came into being as an enterprise as the result of pure necessity and talent, unquestionably underpinned by the alchemy of fusing elements in fire, by the personalities of its founders supported by a great team, and by the unparalleled boldness of marrying popular and aristocratic traditions in the figurines it creates.

Lladró has succeeded in taking what was once a seventeenth-century symbol of European nobility and bourgeoisie to all homes, yet along the way preserving all its fragility, quality, and delicate beauty.

In the forms it borrows from the universe for its works, Lladró reaffirms its defining task of embellishing the world through its unique creations, in contradistinction to the chaotic ugliness with which the world presently regales us.

The Lladró figurines allow us to reinvent reality by means of idealizing a given context with Arcadian gestures. In an emotive tone and with contents divested of intellectual pretenses, they first reach out to the beholder, then retract a little to regain greater depth, ultimately finding their space in the unbridgeable gap, allowing them room to formulate a message of empathy that becomes the brand's guiding rule. Lladró strips the world of its hollow victories and unveils the coexistence of different coordinates of space and time through the expression of the themes depicted in its images. Within the micro-world of a figurine, it regains a discreet subjectivity between the real and the sought-after. Lladró bestows lasting value and meaning on an ephemeral gesture, elevating it to a universal category.

The paradox of the idealized message of simplicity and harmony conveyed by the figurines is that it emerged from a Spain devastated by civil war. The brand's founders were indirect victims of the war's moral and material consequences. And that is how a sense of restlessness and necessity conspired to create a future of splendor nigh impossible to imagine at that time, as if their figurines were the oracular messengers of the success awaiting those children. That is how they began, alternating their work by clearing the scrub from their family orchard with their apprenticeships at a nearby tiles factory.

Fate, necessity, gunpowder, and orange blossom . . .

the story starts in Valencia, a place where the Mediterranean climate created the conditions for the *huerta* (fertile agricultural land). This marvelous and charming oasis, in the midst of hot, arid, and thirsty regions, was made possible by an unsurpassable irrigation system unchanged for centuries. The extreme poverty of the 1940s—as a direct consequence of the war—forced the Lladró brothers to work with their parents in the fields of Almácera near their home, and also to work in a ceramics and tiles factory, decorating plates with simple motifs.

The boys' salary was poor and the work monotonous, but it was there that the artistic interests were brought to life; their mother, Rosa Dolz, had originally stimulated these interests, encouraging them to attend the School of Arts and Crafts.

They worked on their talents during their spare time, making portraits of characters from the *huerta* and drawing the flora and fauna of the coastal marshes. At school, they acquired invaluable knowledge on everything from materials to techniques. This daily work and effort, combined with their innate curiosity and determination, led them to explore and experiment with ceramic techniques.

With the unconditional support of their mother, who encouraged them to stick together, they built a small kiln at home to continue practicing. Their unwavering determination even led them to sell their working oxen in order to buy the fuel they needed to create their first vases, ashtrays, and flowers. While one of the brothers modeled, another painted, and a third fired the pieces in the kiln. The works gradually found buyers in the *huerta*'s neighbors.

Fate appeared when a local factory producing porcelain insulators for electricity lines opened up a china division and contracted the three brothers. This was an excellent opportunity, and they remained there for four years. It also provided a testing ground for experimentation, helping them to learn specific techniques and to develop their artistic skills. After that, they once again ventured out on their own and set up a workshop.

And that was the beginning of the present-day Lladró company. Juan was in charge of decoration, the laboratory, and administrative tasks; Vicente, of glazing, molds, and the kiln; and José, of production and staff liaising.

Both the working hours and the rhythm of production picked up to keep pace with an overwhelming demand for porcelain flowers for ceiling lamps, the first sign of what would be continuous future success for Lladró flowers.

To ensure the sought-after effect of maximum quality, gloss, durability, and all the features of porcelain, they researched the varying proportions of quartz, china clay, and feldspar—the basic ingredients in the composition of porcelain. The brothers also made advances in the construction of the kilns. Given that firing is the last step in the process, the whole work would prove useless if not done to perfection.

Fire was the element with the power to either create or destroy beauty. It was often frustrating to see how a certain piece, technically and artistically splendid before entering the kiln, could collapse if the temperature was not adequate, or perhaps could not achieve the hoped-for quality if it did not reach the maximum temperature the material could tolerate.

In the late 1950s, Adolfo Pucilowsky, a chemist of Polish descent, and the sculptor Fulgencio García joined the project, resulting in a significant boost; they perfected of some aspects in the process of production of the figurines. The skillful hands of the women from the *huerta,* who had modeled the first flowers, had since then been joined by a magnificent team of artists. The Lladró brothers transmitted to their team their exceptional enthusiasm and their highly personal vision of art.

V alencia boasts an extremely rich artistic history, deeply rooted in the Mediterranean tradition. The presence of the great civilizations throughout the centuries has left a mark easily traceable in the everyday signs of a millenary cultural legacy.

The Fallas annual festival is one of the most remarkable and characteristic examples of the impact of art on this land's inhabitants, with hundreds of artisans working throughout the year to create enormous papier-mâché sculptures caricaturing local characters or popular scenes, only to set them on fire every March 19 in the city streets.

In 1727, a center for porcelain production was created in a factory in Alcora, near Valencia, borrowing many of the features of the French style: Bérain, Meissen, Chantilly, and Sèvres. In terms of stylistic receptivity, collaboration between different sculptors, the perfection of its productions, and the mark of prestige bestowed by the possession of one of its pieces, the Alcora factory can be seen as a key precedent of what Lladró represents today.

The early Lladró production was clearly influenced by a more classical tradition. Rural or courtesan scenes, the animal kingdom, and the world of dance were common themes and allowed for a display of technical virtuosity in expression. The lace of the ballerinas' tutus and the almost impossible balance of their steps seem to defy the law of gravity in the firing process, especially if we take into account the unpredictable reaction of porcelain paste to firing.

The subject matter of the figurines represented an idealized world that had a soothing effect on reality. At the time, the general population in Spain lacked basic aesthetic principles. Beauty was seen as a cosmetic trap or as a strategic necessity. And, although the people accepted appetites and exuberance as a connatural element in life, their concept of beauty was conditioned by the prevailing morality of the political regime. The beauty that the working classes discovered by themselves was invisible and closely tied to emotional values, such as companionship, physical strength, and robust health.

An emerging middle class began to regard the ownership of a Lladró figurine as a symbol of beauty and status, following the partiality of some prestigious customers who showed a keen interest in the porcelain of the Lladró brothers. The pieces became signs for protocol, commemorative gifts in weddings, graduations, births, and anniversaries. Customers avidly responded in the first shops in Valencia. Soon, other branches followed, and true expansion began, starting with Lladró's participation in specialized fairs. Again, fate and necessity . . .

In an attempt to differentiate the product and make it more competitive within the market, and after much experimentation, the palette was reduced to a range of grays with beige acting as a counterpoint. This chromatic transformation brought with it a need for a change in form, and it was decided to stylize the figurines in an elongated manner, elevating and instilling in them a sensibility that enhanced their sense of fragileness and beauty.

The exaggerated elongation generally organized the compositions in a vertical arrangement, adding nuances that suggested expressions of ascension, spirituality, security, and strength. Figurines that might have seemed fragile actually acquired a powerful presence. The result was that they become the trademark of the brand, making it easily recognizable in the market.

The figurines appeared more free-flowing, less tense and with an innate grace. They conveyed a sense of calm bordering on abandonment, a languorous, dreamy presence with a hint of absence. The subject matter enhanced the effect of the message. The underlying romanticism stimulated a meeting of mind and heart, producing a timeless and boundless feeling recognizable in all latitudes. Hence the international success.

It is nonetheless paradoxical that Lladró, with its new, successful, subtle, exquisite, fragile, and almost colorless icons became a kind of ambassador for Valencia, a baroque land of floral offerings and fireworks exploding in bursts of colors against the blackness of the night. For that Valencia with its grotesque, sexual, and satirical papier-mâché sculptures, burning in the street in their hundreds every spring during the Fallas festival. For the Valencia inebriated with gunpowder in a celebration of fire and the excess of orange blossom. For the Valencia of costumes with elaborate ornamentation and ample skirts, of colorist gastronomy, of the light shining through in Sorolla's painting.

The factory expanded, and in 1962 it opened a School of Professional Training with official recognition and support. The initiative brought with it a more advanced style of management: the school supplied the company with trained artists. Given their humanist character, the Lladró founding brothers view the workers as a family, in such a way that the tutelage of the company covers specific training as well as specialized medical attention in the company headquarters. The company also organizes documentation and training trips. It has built a sports complex with a gym, swimming pool, and various training tracks for the benefit of employees and their families. Art workshops and computer and language courses, among others, are also offered.

t he company pioneered the incorporation of a large number of women and physically disabled persons into its staff, as well as the scheduling of leisure activities to encourage interaction among all employees. A revolution was thus taking place in the *huerta*, accompanied by an intense interest in creating and maintaining jobs for the inhabitants of the area.

In 1965, Lladró began to focus on the U.S. market, acquiring a distribution network that would be the foundation on which its present-day structure was consolidated. In 1969, the company attended a specialized trade fair in Hannover, followed by others in Sweden, Denmark and Britain. Lladró creations were beginning to be seen in homes all over the world. Entering the international market provided an impressive boost for the company's growth over the following two decades. This led Lladró to design the City of Porcelain, a corporate structure showcasing the increasingly complex creative processes required to create top quality hand-crafted porcelain production. The idea was to put together a rationally organized space without overlooking the fact that it is also a place for creativity and highly delicate handmade work. Particularly striking for its singular architectural differentiation from the rest of the buildings in the City of Porcelain is the sculptors' building. With eyes set on the twenty-firstst century, identical studios were created for each of the artists, all equipped with the same resources yet differentiated by the peculiarities each individual wanted to give them. Models are available on a daily basis so that the artists continually hone their eye-to-hand skills. These spaces have the silence and light necessary for creation, putting dexterity and expertise at the service of porcelain.

t aking an initial idea as a starting point, the sculptor makes a primary sketch in clay that will be the embryo of the new figurine. If it passes the test of the Creativity Committee —currently made up of members of the second generation of the Lladró family and the company's managerial team—the sculptor models it in more detail and at the definitive size, always taking into account the reduction the piece will undergo in the kiln.

The prototype is then submitted to technical analysis. After examining its structure, the experts in this department divide the piece into segments and reproduce each fragment in plaster. After that, the various parts are assembled to form the exact reproduction. This new model is then returned to the sculptor's hands, who will work on it to perfect the tiniest details.

After that, the piece is sent to the decoration department. There, in an atmosphere more akin to monastic elevation, the artists are absorbed in their task, their eyes focusing on what they have in their hands while their gestures create incredible choreographies of micro-movement. Meditative silence and peace prevail. It is here where the piece is decorated following the sculptor's indications, and its still smooth surface is engraved with the delicate motifs that will configure its final aspect. The men and women working in this department come from the Faculty of Fine Arts, from Lladró's own Scholarship Center, or from the School of Arts and Crafts of Valencia. Using the available documentation, they complement the artistic message with the motifs they recreate on the pieces.

Theirs is a virtuous, delicate, and painstaking task, with the pulse of creation moving through their hands. The decorators discover the subtle intersection of the work and its ornamentation, and their dexterity guarantees an expressive balance. Once the decoration is completed, the piece is submitted to a series of tests until achieving final perfection through its firing. The Lladró palette contains more than four thousand tones from which to chose the one best suited to the figurine. The prototype is altered on several occasions until the optimal combination is found. The whole process demands careful attention and a sensibility for detail before receiving the final go-ahead to send the piece to the production workshops.

The porcelain paste flows through underground conduits from the laboratory where the exact formula is created to the three buildings where the molds are filled. Similarly to the rest of the phases in the process, this also demands the utmost concentration and attention to detail, for each figurine may require from fifteen to twenty molds, and even up to three hundred for the more complex pieces. The molds must be filled carefully to avoid air bubbles. After estimating the exact time it needs to set, each segmented piece must be carefully and very gently extracted from the mold in order not to leave prints on the soft paste. The various pieces of the figurines are assembled using liquid porcelain paste as an adhesive. After being meticulously reconstructed, the figurine is then painted to recreate the faces and all the other details that imbue the piece with its expressiveness. And finally it faces the test of fire, with nearly one day in the kiln at more than 1300° C.

The quality control the piece is put through after coming out of the kiln ensures the absolute perfection that merits the Lladró stamp. The piece is then sent to the packaging section.

This complex process also embraces the clear intention of distinguishing the company as an environmentally friendly corporation. Lladró has an active environmental management unit that looks after waste recovery, water recycling, and treatment of waste and gas fluids. The company does everything in its power to raise the awareness of its workers with respect to green issues and concerns.

Defining this company's environmental philosophy and underlying spirit of renewl is the new Re-Cyclos artistic project. In collaboration with designers of international repute, Lladró is elaborating upon an innovative proposal that recovers porcelain pieces from past collections and turns them into ornamental compositions made up with, for instance, Christmas motifs, instilling them with a new order.

The Re-Cyclos initiative is proof of the concerns of a brand undergoing continuous expansion, and not just in commercial terms. Indeed, it is also actively committed to conceptual innovations.

At present, the company's design department includes a team of young professionals endeavoring to introduce Lladró into new fields of interior and fashion design. After all, one of the founding goals of the company was to embellish our private spaces, taking the idea of quality of life as the epitome of true luxury.

Fully committed to this goal of generating quality of life, Lladró continues taking part in solidarity development projects, collaborating with NGOs, for example, in a project aimed at maintaining the sustainable resources in indigenous communities of potters in Mexico.

The alphabet of love . . .

When it comes to the subject matter of its pieces, convention continues being a provocation in itself. The distinction between what is real and what is desirable is dispensed with. All art is an attempt to turn that distinction into something unnatural. Nobody can live a solitary existence with the beauty he or she is capable of perceiving.

Lladró sculptures are figurative and realistic, miniaturized and highly precious. They are bucolic, mythical, fantastic, historical, religious, and literary characters. They are familiar and everyday, like "Linda," a milestone in the brand's history, depicting childhood innocence, a budding flower opening up to emotionality and tenderness.

In the figurines, love always underlies and transmits the flow of life. Above and beyond the space it occupies, every icon enters the realm of time in an attempt to conquer it and turn it into something everlasting.

There is a profusion of animals—horses, elephants, deer, gazelles—in the compositions of figurines and pendants. Another major theme is birds; the flight of birds makes them the ideal symbol of the links between heaven and earth. They are seen as both omens and messages from the heavens. They can also symbolize lightness and freedom from earthly weight, just as angels symbolize superior states of being. The vicinity of coastal lagoons in Valencia, one of Europe's most important nesting areas for aquatic birds, provides Lladró artists with a privileged vantage point for inspiration.

A special mention is deserved for the exquisite and extremely delicate porcelain flowers whose emotive preciousness has made them the best emblem of Lladró's success. Their creation demands the highest dexterity and meticulousness as well as an extreme sensibility in the hands of the workers who make them.

Each petal is individually modeled before use in the overall floral composition with the precision of a mandala. Each flower recreates the irregular edges of petals, and stamens and leaf veins are modeled with the utmost accuracy. The flowers are imbued with exuberance, transparency, and ethereality. Notwithstanding their fragileness and lack of fragrance, their beauty exceeds that of natural flowers since they last over time. Thanks to its undisputed quality and prestige, Lladró is recognized worldwide as a leading brand, a cult product in certain audiences that has led to the creation of a select club of more than one hundred thousand collectors around the world, who enjoy privileges such as being invited to visit the City of Porcelain and the possibility of purchasing exclusive pieces from highly limited series.

In 1988, the Infanta Pilar de Borbón, sister of the King of Spain, opened the Lladró Museum and Gallery in New York, located on Fifty-seventh Street, between Fifth Avenue and Sixth Avenue, in a refurbished 1920s nine-storey building. It houses the exhibition of a large retrospective collection of pieces, the complete collection of figurines of the Collectors Society, and the headquarters of that society on the east coast of the U.S.

The recognition of the exceptional quality of the sculptural pieces of Lladró is readily evident in the fact that they have been put on display in a number of museums, including the State Hermitage Museum in Saint Petersburg, the Museo Nacional de Ceramico González Martí in Valencia, the Musée du Cinquantenaire in Belgium, the International Museum of Ceramics in Faenza, and the Museum of Modern Art of Santo Domingo.

A consolidated network of luxury commercial boutiques was also created in many cities around the world, including Valencia, Madrid, London, New York, Singapore, Hong Kong, and Beverly Hills. This last mentioned is located at 408 Rodeo Drive and encompasses an area of 2,300 square meters. These boutiques are showcases of the ever-evolving sculptures created by artists in the City of Porcelain.

Lladró continues to take on major challenges. Meanwhile, and despite inevitable critical situations, the bond between the brothers has always remained solid, honoring their mother's memory and wishes. The incorporation of members from the second generation of the family onto the Board of Directors and Creativity Committee in 1984 was a way of guaranteeing the continuity of the family business while preserving a policy of permanent change and progress. With a clearly defined project for the future, the second generation joins the path begun by the Lladró founding brothers.

t he theories addressing the inspiration of artists are all projections of the effect that their work has on us when we purchase it. A piece provides us with a glimpse of our past almost as we turn our back on it, or it defines as yet unfulfilled desires. For us, figurines may be a passport to something long yearned for, while their static nature brings a tangible visual harmony which seems to presage future peace. The recognized coexistence of the timeless and the ephemeral in a figurine defines a present emotion that becomes an eternal value.

At present, beyond the apparent evidence, Lladró artists use a fleeting code with a highly spiritual content when interpreting reality in the figurines they mold, rendering any antagonism null and void. True luxury consists in proposing a return to an essential condition, a return that is also a forward march in the consciousness of man's unity.

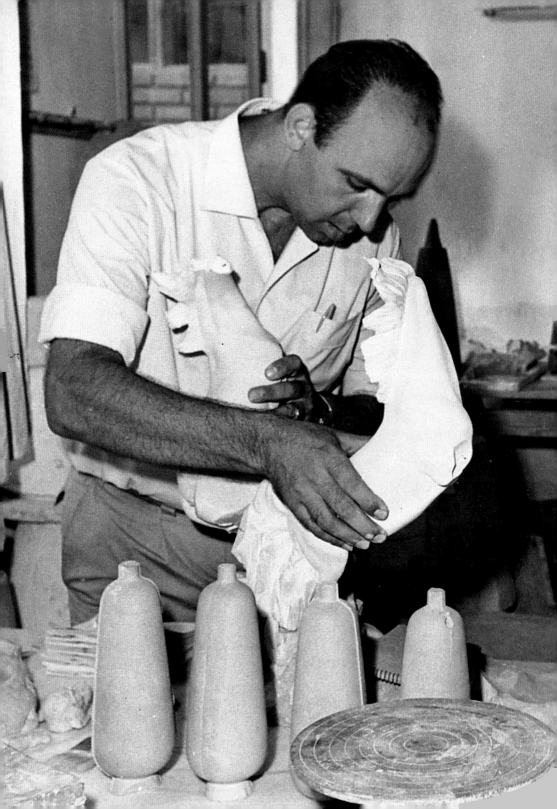

雪裏春前都耐寒深黄
淺絳門江干清涼凡豔
余偁俗繪出憑人苕眼
看
女史惲冰

1. Ángeles Lladró and Michael Douglas.
2. Vicente Lladró and wife, with Julio Iglesias in Miami.
3. Pope John Paul II admiring the *Madonna of Rocío*.
4. H. M. King Juan Carlos I with the founders.
5. Official reception by the king and queen of Spain to the emperor and empress of Japan.
6. Juan Lladró and his wife at the reception offered by the king and queen of Spain to the emperor and empress of Japan.
7. His Imperial Highness Prince Norihito Takamado in front of *Pursued Deer* in the main dining room at his residence, 1996.
8. Michael York in Disney World with the piece *Peter Pan*, 1994.
9. José Lladró with the mayor of New York, 2002.

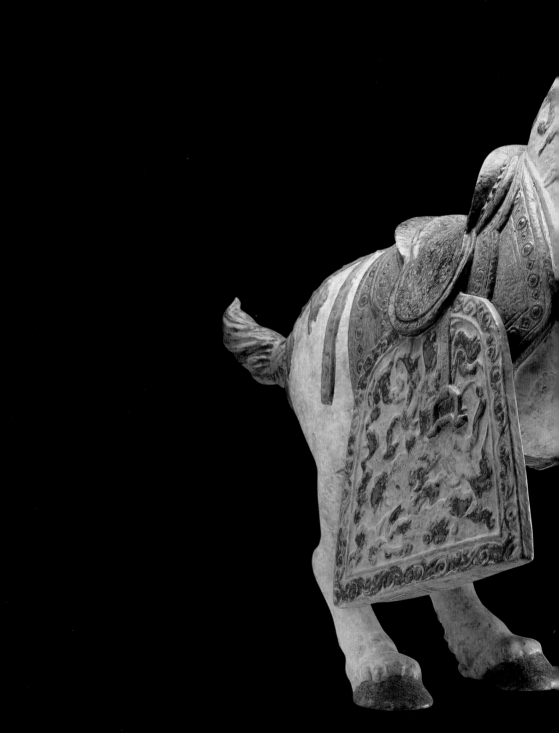

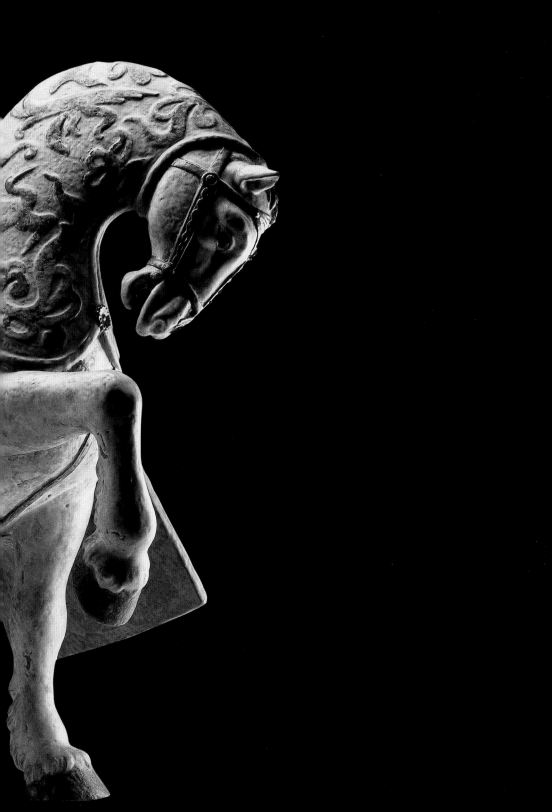

LLADRÓ

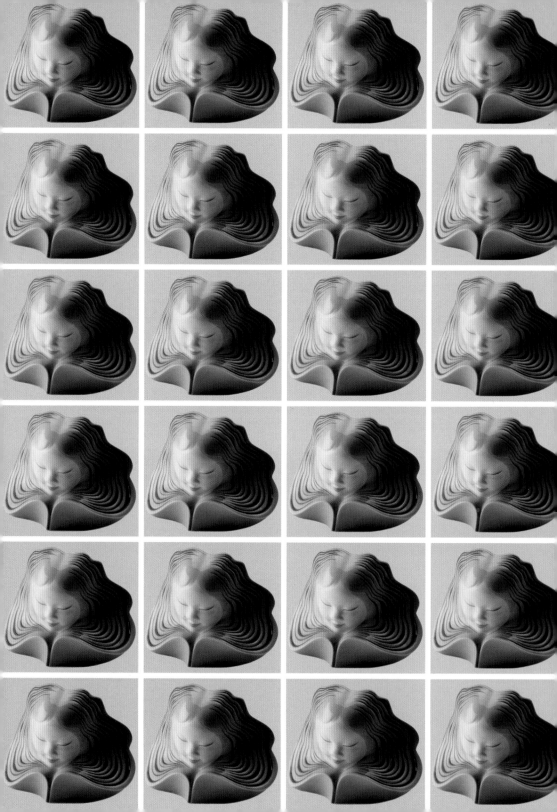

Porcelanas LLADRÓ

EXPOSICION Y VENTA:
PASAJE REX, 8 - TEL. 53702
VALENCIA

FABRICA:
CALLE DE SAN JOSE, 7
ALMACERA (Valencia)

Las piezas catalogadas son: las de mayor aceptación en todos nuestros mercados, por sus modelos y precios altamente comerciales

Catalogue pieces are better in all our best markets because its models and trices are highly comercials

Les piéces cataloguées sont les de meilleur aceptation en touts nos marchés par ses models et prixs hautement commercials

El tamaño se entiende por la altura

Size is by means of the high

Le grandeur is compris par l'hauteur

Número 74
Tam. 21 cms.

Dama con chal
Dame avec schall
Lady with shawl

Número 99
Tam. 10 cms.

Grupo de caza
Groupe de chasse
Hunt's group

Chronology

1953:   The Lladró brothers set off on their artistic career at their family home. They create their first classically inspired figurines.

1958:   Production is transferred to Tavernes Blanques, site of the future City of Porcelain.

1960:   The word "Spain" is added to the Lladró brand as a sign of its dedication to exports.

1962:   Lladró creates the School of Professional Training at the company's headquarters.

1965:   Lladró enters the U.S. market.

1968:   Lladró anticipates current brand diversification strategies and creates Nao.
The company incorporates disabled persons into its staff.

1969:   The first installations at the City of Porcelain are opened.
The presentation of *Sad Harlequin* with its moving gesture and stylized lines marks an important shift in the artistic evolution of the firm.

1970:   Lladró introduces its first pieces in gres, a material with earthy tones that opens up new expressive possibilities.

1971:   The range of vases appears, proving an excellent showcase for Lladró painters.

1973:   Lladró strengthens its presence in the American market by buying 50 percent of Weil Ceramics & Glass.

1974:   The emblematic blue identifier of the Lladró brand starts to be used with a stamp on the base of the figurines.
The Elite Collection is born, comprising pieces elaborated with special attention to detail.

1976:   *Playing Cards* is issued, the first gres piece in the Elite Collection.

1983:   *Flowers of the Season* is a composition replete with flowers. With this piece, Lladró incorporates what would be a characteristic element of signature quality: floral compositions sculpted petal by petal. This piece breaks all records in sales for Lladró.

1984:   The three Lladró brothers open the door to the future with the incorporation into the company of one child per founder: Rosa, Mamen, and Juan Vicente Lladró.
The sculptors' building is built at the City of Porcelain.

1985:   Birth of the Lladró Collectors' Society, which in the fifteen years since its creation has brought together more than one hundred thousand lovers of Lladró porcelain.

1986:   The subsidiary Bussan Lladró is created in Tokyo.
That same year, the Chinese subsidiary Disvasa-Pacific Ltd is set up in Hong Kong.

Vase n°4, *1958, made and decorated by José Lladró.*
© *Daisa.*

1988:   Lladró consolidates its expansion into the Anglo-Saxon market, setting up the subsidiaries Lladró UK, Ltd., Ordal Australia, and Lladró USA.
Opening of the Lladró Museum of New York on Fifty-seventh Street in Manhattan.

1991:   The Saint George Room at the Hermitage Museum of San Petersburg hosts an exhibition of Lladró sculptures. Since then, *18th Century Coach* and *Don Quixote* have been part of its permanent collection.
Lladró set up its subsidiary in Singapore, Disvasa (Singapore) Pte. Ltd.

1993:   Lladró receives the Prince of Asturias Award for Internationalization.

1994:   The Museum of Modern Art of Santo Domingo organizes a monographic exhibition titled *Lladró de cerca* (Lladró up close). *Spirit of America* is added to the museum's permanent collection.

1996:   The Lladró Center in Madrid opens with an event presided over by many of the city's leading authorities.

1997:   Lladró receives the Prince of Asturias Award for Competitiveness.
The Lladró Centre in Beverly Hills opens at number 408 on the mythical North Rodeo Drive. The building was jointly designed by the architects Juan Vicente Lladró, Rafael Tamarit, and Ki Suh Park.

1999:   The Legend Collection is created, combining porcelain with gold and precious stones.
The Lladró Center opens in Las Vegas. It is situated in the spectacular Venetian Hotel casino.

2000:   Lladró becomes the first Spanish company to win a lawsuit in China against piracy, halting the production of a factory and confiscating the casts used to forge the pieces.
Lladró sets up its subsidiary in Italy, Lladró Italia Srl.
The Lladró Center opens in Sydney, Australia.

2001:   Lladró Privilege replaces the Lladró Collectors Society.
Lladró takes a major stake in the jewelry brand Carrera y Carrera.

2002:   Lladró receives the Prince of Asturias Award for Development of a Leading Brand.

2003:   The three founding brothers hand over control to the second generation of Lladró. Since then, they have been represented proportionally on the Board of Directors by two children each. Incorporation of younger members of the second generation includes David, Ángeles, and María José Lladró.

2004:   The three Lladró families agree to trust executive management to a CEO and managing director with recognized experience in international luxury brands. Alain Viot leaves the Richemont Group to take up the post.

2005:   Lladró sponsors the China Team in the America's Cup, to be held in Valencia in 2007. Lladró is the first company from Valencia to sponsor a team in the 32nd America's Cup.
Lladró and Supergrif sign a collaboration agreement to launch the first collection of the new Lladró Bath line.

2006:   Lladró acquires 100 percent of the capital and control of the jewelry group Carrera y Carrera.

Vase n°2, 1958, made and decorated by José Lladró.
© *Daisa.*

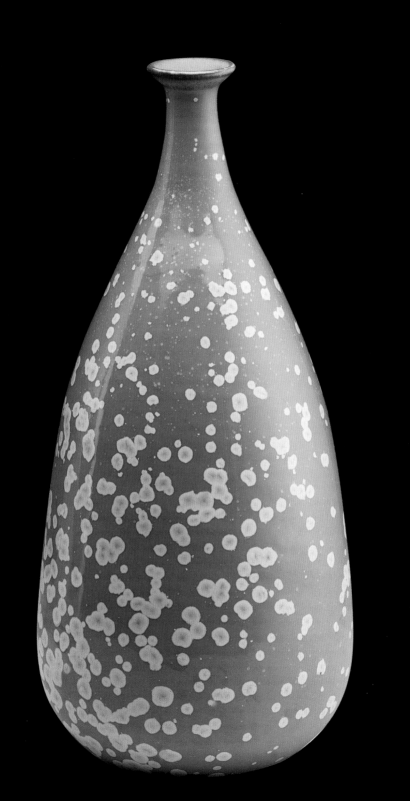

LLADRÓ®

José Lladró composing a piece at his first workshop in the house in Almácera. © Lladró.
Vase n°3, 1953, decorated by crystallizations by José Lladró. © Daisa.

Urn (Lady with Rose), 1940, crowned by a sculpture made by Vicente Lladró and painted by his brother José. © Daisa.
Portrait of Marie Antoinette Archduchess of Austria in 1769, Joseph Ducreux (Palace of Versailles). © Gérard Blot/RMN.

Magno Red Vase, 1972, with decoration inspired by oriental lacquers. © Daisa.
Flowers and Insects, illustrated album on ten leafs by Nu Shi Yun Bing, Musée Guimet, Paris. © Guimet, dist RMN/Ghislain Vanneste.

A view of the classrooms of the School of Arts and Crafts of Valencia, at the time when the brothers were studying there. © Lladró.

Clay sketch by the sculptor Fulgencio García. © Daisa.
Vaslav Nijinski, member of Giaghelev's Ballets Russes, starring here in the latter's classical ballet, *Le Spectre de la Rose*, c. 1910. © Bettmann/Corbis.

José Lladró and Manuel González Martí, a scholar of Valencia's artistic and handcrafted tradition, and founder of the National Museum of Ceramics of Valencia, visiting the production line. © Lladró.

Pheasant (head lowered) and *Pheasant (head raised)*, 1968, refined and expressive lines. © Daisa.

1. Ángeles Lladró and Michael Douglas. 2. Vicente Lladró and wife with Julio Iglesias in Miami. 3. Pope John Paul II admiring the *Madonna of Rocío*. 4. H. M. King Juan Carlos I with the founders. 5. Official reception by the king and queen of Spain to the emperor and empress of Japan. 6. Juan Lladró and his wife at the reception offered by the king and queen of Spain to the emperor and empress of Japan. 7. His Imperial Highness Prince Norihito Takamado in front of *Pursued Deer* in the main dining room at his residence, 1996. 8. Michael York in Disney World with the piece *Peter Pan*, 1994. 9. José Lladró with Michael R. Bloomberg, mayor of New York, 2002. © Lladró.

Vicente Lladró presenting the Lladró FIFA Trophy, 1973. © Lladró.

Oriental Horse, 1971, limited series of 350 units made in gres, a material making it possible to work in large formats. © Daisa.

Craftswomen in the painting department. © Lladró.

Polar Bear, 1965. © Daisa.

One of the many interpretations of Don Quixote by Lladró, 1986, this time in gres, a design by sculptor Pablo Serrano. © Daisa.

"It was yet early in the morning, at which time the sunbeams did not prove so offensive": illustration by Gustave Doré, engraved on wood by H. Pisan, in the first French translation of *Don Quijote* by Miguel de Cervantès Saavedra, 1863. © BNF.

Horses' Group, matt porcelain, 1969. © Daisa.

Panoramic view of the City of Porcelain, and view of the sculptors' building.
© Lladró.

Permanent exhibition room at the City of Porcelain. © Lladró.
First Lladró stand at the Valencia trade fair. © Lladró.

Lladró headquarters in Beverly Hills. © Lladró.
From top to bottom: boutique Lladró Madrid; façade of Beverly Hills boutique;
boutique Lladró Barcelona. © Lladró.

Water Baby Vase, 1989. © Daisa.
The singular beauty of materials born from the earth. © Lladró.

Lladró styles. © Daisa.
One of the first catalogues used by the Lladró brothers to show their creations.
© Lladró.

Juan Lladró with mayor of New York, Edward I. Koch, 1988. © Lladró.

Juan Lladró decorating some pieces at the workshop of their family home. © Lladró.
From top to bottom: the Lladró brothers with George H. W. Bush; José Lladró and Martin Luther King, Jr. in a studio observing a sculptor making an image of Martin Luther King, Jr.; José Lladró painting a piece next to Anne of Orléans, Duchess of Calabria. © Lladró.

Modelling workshop at the brothers' family home. © Lladró.

Lyric Muse, 1971, a large format (114 cm) gres piece, limited series of four hundred units. © Daisa.
Sad Harlequin, 1969, prototype of a style created in the late 1960s, characteristic for the extreme stylization of figurines and grey and beige tones contrasting with white. © Daisa.

Vaslav Nijinski in *Le Dieu Bleu*, 1912, with music by Reynaldo Hahn, choreography by Michel Fokine, plot by Jean Cocteau and Federico de Madrazo, and costumes by Léon Bakst. © Rue des Archives.
The Blue God, 1982, as an homage to Vaslav Nikinski. © Daisa.

Aura Collection, 2003, exhibition at the Ludwig Mies van der Rohe pavilion in Barcelona, 2005. © Daisa.

Harlequin, Utopía Collection, 2006. A revision of a classic. © Daisa.
Composition of the first *Re-Cyclos* Collection, 2005. © Daisa.

Board of directors, present day. © Lladró.